The Various Twist to Pretzels

Different Knots for You to Intertwine!

BY: Ivy Hope

Copyright © 2020 by Ivy Hope

Copyright/License Page

Please don't reproduce this book. It means you are not allowed to make any type of copy (print or electronic), sell, publish, disseminate or distribute. Only people who have written permission from the author are allowed to do so.

This book is written by the author taking all precautions that the content is true and helpful. However, the reader needs to be careful about his/her action. If anything happens due to the reader's actions the author won't be taken as responsible.

Table of Contents

Introduction 6

   Dreamy Delight 8

   The Easter Save 11

   The Honey, Ham, and Swiss Knot 14

   The Dog Knots 16

   A Spicy Perspective 19

   The Unconventional Pretzels 22

   A British Twist 24

   The Perfect Knot 28

   The Jalapeño Delight 31

   Your Favorite Pretzel 34

   The Simple Knot 37

   The Heavenly Knot 40

   Pretzels for Diet 44

   A Perfect Dinner Knot 47

PB&J Sand- Nah! PB & Honey Bites 50

The Classic Cookie Knot 53

Coco Pretzels 56

Pudding with A Twist 59

The Rollers 62

Keto bites 65

The Vegan's Pick 67

Breakfast Bites 70

Vegan Heart 73

The Herbal Knot 76

The Perfect Appetizer 79

The Big Delight 81

Mini Coco Bites 84

The Classic Cheese Pretzel 86

Pretzel Pie 89

Pretzel cake 92

Conclusion 94

About the Author 95

Author's Afterthoughts... 96

Introduction

Pretzels are one of the best snacks, originated in Italy, and everyone around the World enjoys the delight. It is not that surprising, though. After all, pretzels have quite a divine history. From being invented by a monk for Lent, it is now a reward for children who memorized their prayers. These delights are a true savior in terms of snacks; this statement could be said both- literally and figuratively!

There is so much history to this simple and easy baked snack! However, that is not why it is adored by everyone. Pretzels are preferred for their sweet and salty flavor, heightened by their soft or sometimes hard texture. This is why they are so special. Pretzels have so many different variations to them, and none would ever leave you feeling beaten (pun intended.)

Desiring something that is soft and doughy? Bake some soft pretzels with the help of this cookbook comprising 30 lip-smacking pretzel recipes. And baking them isn't a very tough task. Just put your aprons on and follow the instructions and let your inside chef come out and don't hesitate to make your loved ones happy. Get ready to please everyone!

Dreamy Delight

Whenever someone thinks about Bacon and cheese, it is always as a sandwich. A classic snack for every foodie out there! However, being a foodie also entails one important and personally, one of the most gratifying traits- We can eat anything as long as it has bacon and cheese in it. However, with this recipe, you are sure to forget about all the other bacon and cheese combos! Because, what can be more satisfying than bacon and cheese all stuffed into a pretzel bun?!

Ingredients

- Milk -16 ounces (2 cups)
- Active dry yeast - 4 tsp
- Brown sugar - 2-3 ounces
- Butter - 2 ounces (melted)
- Refined flour - 4 cups
- Fine salt - 2 tsp
- Crushed bacon - 1 pound
- Shredded cheddar cheese - 1 pint
- Baking soda - 5 tablespoon
- Warm water - 2 cups
- Butter - 6 tbsp
- Smoked paprika - 0.04 oz
- Fresh herbs - 2 tsp
- Clove of garlic minced - 1
- Coarse salt - 2 tsp

Serving Size: 6

Preparation time: 30 minutes

Instructions

1. Heat the stove up to 110°, and warm the milk just a little. Use a microwave if required.

2. Add yeast and stir, before letting it rest for approximately three minutes. Add sugar and butter along with the flour. Pour the flour in intervals of one cup at a time and finally add salt.

3. Knead the mixture with a mixer or you can use your hand. Put the dough in a bowl and cover it with a moist cloth. Let it rest for an hour, or until the dough is increased in size.

4. Now, preheat the oven to 400°.

5. Punch into and soften the dough. Then, make 12 divisions of the dough and flatten the lumps into 6 cm wide disks. Add cheese and crushed bacon into these disks, as per requirement, and properly pinch it close.

6. Dip each of these rolls into a bowl filled with baking soda and warm water.

7. Now put these rolls on an oiled baking slip, sprinkle coarse salt. Using a serrated knife, cut slits on the upper part of every roll. Put them in the oven and bake them for 15 minutes.

8. Mix paprika and garlic in the melted butter. Add herbs if required into this mixture. Smear the baked rolls with this once they are taken out of the oven.

9. Have them when they are hot!

The Easter Save

Easter, one of the most anticipated holidays. And, why wouldn't it be? It is a day of great importance. A day wherein the whole family comes together to celebrate. That, however, also entails that it is a day where food is of utmost importance as well. With your whole family gathered at your home, this pretzel recipe is the best choice to highlight your cooking skills. As for the ones away from your family, cheer yourself up by baking these adorable bunny-shaped pretzels- you deserve it!

Ingredients

- Warm water - 2 pints
- Salt - 1 tsp
- Sugar - 2-2 ½ tsp
- Active dry yeast - 0.3-ounce
- Refined flour - 2 ¼ cups
- Baking soda - 1.5 ounce
- Butter(unsalted) melted - 1-ounce
- Egg yolk- 1

Serving Size: 6

Preparation time: 20 minutes

Instructions

1. Mix salt and sugar in a bowl of warm water. In this mixture, add yeast and let it rest for 5 minutes.

2. In the stand mixer, add flour into melted butter and mix at low speed. Once the dough is somewhat mixed into one, increase the speed to medium and continue till the dough has softened.

3. Using vegetable oil, lather a bowl with it and put the dough into the bowl. Cover the bowl for 1 hour or until the time the dough is raised to double its original height.

4. Make small divisions of the dough and roll them to oval-shaped buns.

5. Preheat the oven at 450°F.

6. Boil some water in a pan and add baking soda into it. Now, carefully dip the pretzels into this liquid mix, one batch at a time, and let them rest for 30 seconds.

7. Line the baking sheet with a parchment paper and place the pretzels on top of it. Using a kitchen shear, cut 2 ears into the pretzels.

8. Separate the egg yolk and beat it well. Brush each pretzel with the egg yolk and bake for around 8- minutes or until golden brown.

9. Remove the pretzels and add eyes using an edible marker.

10. Serve!

The Honey, Ham, and Swiss Knot

When we think about having a heavy breakfast or lunch, what is the first thing that comes to our mind? A sandwich, right? And, when it comes to sandwiches, ham, and cheese has always been an easy pick. So, why not upgrade the sandwich up by a notch. Now, satisfy your cravings for ham and cheese with a twist of honey, all put together with a pretzel! This delicious combo is sure to amaze you and everyone around you, and it is super easy to make as well!

Ingredients

- Frozen pretzels – 4, or as required
- Deli ham – 4, taken in the same amount as the pretzel
- Swiss cheese - 8 slices
- Unsalted Butter – 1 oz
- Honey mustard – 4 tbsp, proportionate to ham used
- Serving Size: 4

Preparation time: 10 minutes

Instructions

1. Take the frozen pretzels and thaw them. Now, cut these pretzels into half and spread the honey mustard on the bottom slice of the pretzel. For every pretzel, use two slices of cheese and one of ham. Put the upper layer after adding the cheese and ham.

2. Melt the butter and mix the packed salt present in the pretzel pack. Brush this mix over the pretzel.

3. Heat the griddle and smear the top of the griddle with butter.

4. Grill the pretzels on each side until the cheese has melted.

5. Serve Hot!

The Dog Knots

Hotdogs are the one thing that everyone picks when they do not have time to cook up something delicious. But, why leave the poor hot dogs in such an excluded condition when you could turn them into something absolutely delicious. With this recipe, you are sure to pick hotdogs over any other regular breakfast of yours. Mixing pretzel, a universally loved food item, with hotdogs, is the best decision a man could have ever made! Was that an exaggeration? Maybe! But, is the statement false in any way? Decide for yourself by cooking up this delicious mix of pretzel and hotdogs for your breakfast, or lunch, or even dinner!

Ingredients

- Warm water – 1 cup
- Sugar – 2 tsp
- Koshering salt – 1 tsp
- Active dry yeast – 1 ½ tsp
- Flour – 10 oz
- Butter melted – 1 tbsp
- Mineral water – 10 cups
- Cooking oil - 2 tbsp
- Baking soda – 3 oz
- Beaten egg yolk with 1 tbsp of water
- Coarse salt for pretzel - 1 pack
- Hot dogs – 8

Serving Size: 8

Preparation time: 20 minutes

Instructions

1. In a bowl, mix the koshering salt, sugar, and water. Place the bowl in the mixer and add yeast to the mixture. Whip it well for around five minutes.

2. Add butter and flour in the mix and put the mixer on low. Increase the speed to medium once the mix is combined enough and continue for five minutes or till the dough is kneaded properly.

3. Now, put the dough in a bowl smeared with oil. Wrap the bowl with plastic and let the dough sit for around 50-55 minutes.

4. Preheat the oven to 450°F. Take a baking sheet and line it with baking paper smeared with the cooking oil.

5. Divide the batter equally into eight parts. Stretch and roll the dough. Now, flatten these rolls and place a hotdog in each of this flattened dough. Wrap up the hotdog with the dough and roll it close.

6. Boil water in a pan and add baking soda to it.

7. For 30 seconds, dip each of these rolls in boiling water. Remove them and place them on the parchment paper.

8. Brush these rolls with the liquefied egg yolk and shower the packed salt on top of them.

9. Place the sheet containing the rolls into the oven and bake for 15 minutes or until golden brown. Take out once done and place them on a dish.

10. Serve hot!

A Spicy Perspective

A normal pretzel is absolutely lovely! We all love it. But, imagine pretzels smeared with honey and sprinkled with Sriracha salt! A snack which you can have when your whole family is around, or when you are alone and binge-watching all your favorite movies and series. These pretzels are sure to provide your taste buds a sweet yet spicy kick!

Ingredients

- Warm water – 3 cups
- Sugar – 3 tsp
- Active dry yeast – 2 ½ tsp
- Sea Salt (Himalayan Salt) – 2 tsp
- Honey – 3 oz
- Refined flour – 4 ½ cups
- Butter(melted) – 6 tbsp
- Egg wash (3 tbsp water + egg yolk)
- Sriracha Salt - 2 tsp
- Water – 6 pints (to boil)
- Baking soda – 3.4 oz

Serving Size: 12

Preparation time: 40 minutes

Instructions

1. Preheat the oven to 450°F.

2. Mix sugar and warm water in a bowl and add yeast in it. Let it sit for approximately ten minutes. In a stand mixer, add the flour, honey, melted butter, and the Himalayan salt. Mix on low, and gradually increase the speed to medium once the dough is kneaded enough. Cover the bowl with a wrap, and let it rest for 60 minutes.

3. Take the dough and divide it into 6 equally pieced stripes. Elongate the strips into ten inches long ropes and separate each rope from the middle. Make a pretzel-shaped knot using them.

4. In a pan, boil 6 pints of water with baking soda mixed in it. On the side, take a baking sheet and line it with parchment paper.

5. Dip the pretzel carefully into the boiling water for 30 seconds. Later, place these pretzels on the baking sheet and smear the egg wash on every individual knot. Sprinkle the Sriracha on top of these pretzels. Place each batch separately into the oven.

6. Bake for 15 minutes or until the pretzels turn golden brown. Let them cool after.

7. Serve!

The Unconventional Pretzels

A pretzel recipe that requires the least amount of ingredients is easy to cook up and will just turn out to be the best snack you have ever made! These small bites are sure to be the one you cook up so often when you get the undeniable craving for midnight snacks because they are delicious, and they don't even take that long to be made! What can sound better than that? Nothing!

Ingredients

- Synder's pretzels (Hard dough) – 12 oz
- Cooking oil – 2 oz
- Yellow Mustard – 2 tbsp
- Onion Powder – 1 tsp
- Honey – 2.5 oz

Serving Size: 6

Preparation time: 5 minutes

Instructions

1. In a bowl, mix the yellow mustard, onion powder, cooking oil and honey.

2. Crush the pretzels into small pieces and add them to the above-made mix.

3. Preheat the oven to 275°F.

4. Take a baking sheet and place a parchment paper on it. Spread the pretzels onto the baking sheet and even them out.

5. Place the sheet in the oven and bake for half an hour. During this process, keep turning the pretzels over between certain time intervals.

6. After removing them, let them cool.

7. Serve!

A British Twist

Fried fish is most probably everyone's personal favorite. This classy food item is picked every time and by every person of every age group. So, when you have your family coming over for dinner, and you don't have much time to cook up something elegant looking, you can definitely settle for this pretzel dish! Because who would not love to have fish stuffed between the delicious and soft pretzel buns? Even if someone does not, you can always give them fried fish and pretzels separately. There is no negative point to this recipe, and that's for sure!

Ingredients

For fish fillets:

- Firm tofu – 1
- Mild curry powder – ¼ tsp
- Panko flakes – 3 oz
- Lemon zest – 1 tsp
- Dried dill – ¼ tsp
- Salt – ¼ tsp
- Refined flour – 2 tbsp
- Paprika powder – 2 tsp
- Dried seaweed – 1/3 sheet
- Water – ¼ cup
- Vegetable oil - 2 tbsp
- Salt – ½ tsp

For pretzel buns:

- Refined flour – 2 ½ cups
- Olive oil – 1 tsp
- Water – 1 cup
- Baking soda – 2 tsp
- Instant yeast – 1 tsp
- Salt – ½ tsp
- Pretzel salt – 1 tsp
- Lettuce leaves - 1 cup

For Garlic yogurt sauce:

- Salt - 2 tsp
- Garlic clove – 1
- Chopped dill – 1
- Unsweetened soy yogurt – ½ cup

Serving Size: 4

Preparation time: 45 minutes

Instructions

For fish fillet:

1. Mix 1 ounce of water with flour and add half teaspoon of salt into the mix, to make a liquid-like consistency. For the breadcrumbs, add dried dills, panko flakes, curry and paprika powder, lemon zest, crushed dried seaweed, and salt.

2. Squeeze out the excess water from the tofu. Slice the tofu into four divisions.

3. Dip each piece of tofu into the flour and water mix. Take this tofu and place them on the breadcrumbs and cover them with it.

4. Pour olive oil into a frying pan. In this pan, add the tofu slices and fry them until they are crispy and golden brown.

For pretzel buns:

1. Preheat the oven to 480°F.

2. In a bowl, mix flour, salt, active dry yeast, and olive oil along with 250 ml warm water. Run the stand mixer on medium till the dough is softened.

3. Once the dough has been kneaded, let it rest for 60 minutes or till it doubles in size.

4. Remove the dough and make 4 divisions of it.

5. In a pan, add water and baking soda and let it boil. Dip each of these rolls in the boiling water for 30 seconds.

6. Make a slit on the top of each roll and sprinkle it with pretzel salt.

7. Line a baking sheet with parchment paper and place these rolls on top of it. Put them into the oven and bake them for approximately 20 minutes or till they turn golden brown.

For the garlic yogurt sauce:

1. Mix the unsweetened soy yogurt, crushed garlic clove, salt and chopped dill in a bowl.

For assembling:

1. Cut the pretzel rolls in two equal parts. On the bottom place a few leaves of lettuce and top it with the fried fish.

2. Add the garlic yogurt sauce on top and press the bun close.

The Perfect Knot

Want to make the perfect pretzel? Although a regular pretzel does not sound so bad, imagine having a pretzel with brie cheese, sea salt, and rosemary in it. The combination is so good that it will leave you wanting more! And why wouldn't it? Just the thought of pulling apart a soft, cheesy pretzel that has rosemary and sea salt ever so generously sprinkled over it, while watching as the brie cheese stretches into those delicious strings and the scent of rosemary wafts into your surroundings, is enough to make one run straight to the kitchen to bake these godly pretzels.

Ingredients

- Butter (melted) – 2 oz
- Sliced Brie cheese – 7 oz
- Warm water – 2 ½ cups
- Sugar – 1 tbsp
- Sea Salt – 2 tsp
- Flour – 4 ½ cups
- Water – 4 pints
- Instant yeast – 2 ¼ tsp
- Olive oil - 2 tbsp
- Baking soda – 2.25 oz
- Fresh rosemary - 2 tbsp
- Sea salt - 2 tsp

Serving Size: 8

Preparation time: 80 minutes

Instructions

1. Preheat the oven 425°F.

2. Mix water, sugar, yeast and salt in a bowl, then let it sit for five minutes. Now, add in butter and flour into the bowl and work the stand mixer on low for around five minutes or until the dough has mixed enough to be pulled off from the bowl's surface.

3. Smear another bowl with oil and place the dough into it. Cover the bowl with a wrap and let it rest for 60 minutes or till the dough doubles in its size.

4. Place the dough on a surface sprinkled with flour and slice it into 8 divisions. Elongate them into eighteen inches long thick thread-like structures by rolling them on the floured surface.

5. Now, slightly press them flat on the surface and add the brie cheese along its length. Pinch them close and roll each of the pieces to completely enclose the cheese in the dough. Twist them carefully into a pretzel knot.

6. In a pan, boil water mixed with baking soda. Meanwhile, take 2 baking sheets and line them with parchment paper.

7. Dip each of the pretzels in the pan for half a minute. After removing them, place them on the baking sheet and smear olive oil on each of the pretzels. Sprinkle rosemary and sea salt over them.

8. Bake for 15 minutes or until they turn golden brown.

9. Serve hot!

The Jalapeño Delight

Stuffed pretzels are always great. No matter what the stuffing is, we are bound to love them. But pretzels stuffed with cream cheese and a delicious mix of spices, including jalapeño sound just about perfect. These chewy treats will provide your taste buds with a flavor that they will never be able to forget. They are the perfect snacks for when you crave something cheesy yet spicy!

Ingredients

- Instant yeast – 1 packet
- Salt – 2 tsp
- Sugar – 2 ½ tbsp
- Refined flour – 5 cups
- Red pepper flakes(crushed) – 1 tsp
- Melted Butter(unsalted) – 3 oz
- Water – 2 ½ cups
- Shredded cheese – 1 ½ cup
- Cream cheese – 1 ½ cup
- Coarse sea salt - 2 tsp
- Garlic powder – 1 tsp
- Chopped green chilies – 2 tbsp
- Crumbled bacon – 3 strips
- Egg wash – 3 oz baking soda, 10 cups water, and 1 egg

Serving Size: 8

Preparation time: 80 minutes

Instructions

1. Preheat the oven to 425°F.

2. In a bowl mix salt, yeast and sugar with three cups of flour. Pour in water along with butter. Keep the stand mixer at a lower speed, and with an interval add another cup and a half of flour into the bowl. Add more if the mix is still watery. Now, increase the speed from low to medium and continue for 5 minutes, or until the dough is able to be pulled away from the bowl's surface.

3. Place the dough in a greased bowl. Cover the bowl with a wrap and let it rest for 60 minutes.

4. Mix the red pepper flakes, garlic powder, jalapeño and chilies with cream cheese. Add crumbled bacon and shredded cheese into this mix and combine well.

5. In a pan, boil water mixed in with baking soda. Meanwhile, take a baking sheet and line it with parchment paper.

6. Sprinkle flour on a surface and place the dough on top of it. Make eight equal divisions of the dough and roll these pieces into a long rope. Flatten these ropes and put the previously made filling into them. Pinch the piece close and roll them back into a cylindrical shape. Carefully twist them into a pretzel knot.

7. Dip these knots in the boiling water for 30 seconds.

8. Place these knots on the baking sheet and smear the egg wash over them, sprinkling them with shredded cheese and salt after.

9. Place them into the oven for 14 minutes or till they turn golden brown.

10. Let them rest for around five minutes and serve!

Your Favorite Pretzel

We all love a cheesy pizza. The satisfaction of biting cheese-topped dough is something that always brings a smile to everyone's face. So, why not add that aspect into a pretzel to make the perfect snack for your inner kid. Whip out your baking sheet and set the timer on your oven. You have an important snack to bake!

Ingredients

- Butter(melted) – 3 tbsp
- Marinara sauce – ½ cup
- Chopped pepperoni – 2 oz
- Dough (pizza) – 1 pack
- Cheddar cheese – ½ cup
- Sugar – 2 tbsp
- Baking soda – 1.2 oz
- Coarse salt - 2 tsp

Serving Size: 4

Preparation time: 80 minutes

Instructions

1. Preheat the oven to 350°F.

2. Sprinkle a surface with flour and place the dough on top of it. Now, make eight equal divisions of the dough. Cut these eight divisions into further halves to get sixteen rolls.

3. Flatten these rolls and add 2 tablespoons of cheese, 1 tablespoon of marinara sauce and 1 tablespoon of crushed pepperoni. Brush the edges with water and pinch close.

4. Take a baking sheet and line it with parchment paper.

5. In a pan, boil water mixed with baking soda and sugar. Dip the rolls in this boiling water for 30 seconds.

6. Place the rolls on top of the baking sheet and smear butter on top of each roll. Sprinkle the rolls with salt.

7. Place these rolls in the oven for 15 minutes or until they have turned golden brown.

8. Serve hot!

The Simple Knot

Craving for something normal once in a while is normal! We all have those times when we need something that is simple, and yet, can satisfy our cravings. That is exactly why this recipe is the one you should keep with you at all times! Now, these pretzels may be simple, but they are far from being mediocre!

Ingredients

- Bread Flour – 4 cups
- Melted butter(unsalted) – 5 tbsp
- Kosher salt – 2 ½ tsp
- Warm water – 1 cup
- Brown sugar – 2 tbsp
- Active dry yeast – 1 pack
- Baking soda – ¾ cup
- Water – 12 cups
- Canola Oil – 1 tsp
- Coarse sea salt - 2 tsp

Serving Size: 8

Preparation time: 80 minutes

Instructions

1. Preheat the oven to 425°F.

2. Mix the flour, water, sugar, butter, and yeast in a stand mixer. Sprinkle in salt and blend at low till the dough has combined a bit. Gradually increase the speed to medium and continue until the dough stops sticking to the bowl's surface.

3. Put the kneaded dough in a bowl smeared with oil. Cover with a wrap and let it rest for 60 minutes or until the dough has doubled in size.

4. Take a baking sheet and line it with parchment paper. Meanwhile, boil some water in a pan mixed with baking soda.

5. Sprinkle some flour on the counter and put the dough on it. Divide the dough into eight equal parts. Roll each of these divisions into a 20-inch long rope and shape them into a pretzel knot.

6. Now, dip these knots in the boiling water for 30 seconds. Then, place them on the baking sheet and sprinkle them with the coarse sea salt.

7. Put them into the oven and bake them for around 15 minutes or until they have turned golden brown.

8. Let the pretzels rest for a while. Serve warm!

The Heavenly Knot

Who doesn't love caramelized apples? That sweet taste of apple intensified by the caramel that it is so generously mixed with. This recipe brings you just that, with a twist, you may never be able to forget! This pretzel recipe will give you the most heavenly combo of caramelized apple and cheese. Enjoy the taste of sweetness and sourness mixed together perfectly in a pretzel through this recipe!

Ingredients

For Filling:

- Brown Sugar – ½ tbsp
- Butter(unsalted) – 1 tbsp
- Apples – 2
- Shredded cheese – ¾ cup
- Cinnamon – ¼ tsp.

For Pretzels:

- Kosher salt – ¾ tsp
- Brown sugar – 1 tbsp
- Warm water – ¾ cup
- Soft Wheat Flour – 2 ¼ cups
- Active dry yeast – 1 ½ tsp
- Butter(unsalted) – ¼ cup
- Water – 3 quarts
- Baking soda – 3 oz
- egg wash - 1
- Coarse sea salt - 2 tsp
- Canola oil - 2 tbsp

For the Sauce:

- Brown sugar – ½ cup
- Heavy cream – 1/3 cup
- Butter(unsalted) – 2 tbsp
- Apple cider – 1 cup

Serving Size: 4

Preparation time: 30 minutes

Instructions

1. Preheat the oven to 425°F.

2. In the stand mixer, combine the yeast and brown sugar in water. Let it rest for five minutes, and then add soft wheat flour, salt, and brown sugar into the mix. Combine on low speed. Increase the speed once the dough has combined enough to medium. Mix the dough for further 5 minutes, or until the dough pulls away from the bowl's surface.

3. Place this dough in a bowl smeared with oil. Cover with plastic wrap and let it rest for 60 minutes.

4. Start preparing for the filling around 15 minutes before the 60 minute ends. For the filling, cook the sliced apples with butter, a pinch of cinnamon and brown sugar in a pan on medium heat till the apples have caramelized.

5. Sprinkle some flour on the surface. Place the dough on it and make 4 equal divisions of it. Flatten these divisions into circles. Put the cheddar cheese and caramelized apples on it. Then, brush the corners with the egg yolk and carefully pinch it close.

6. Take a baking sheet and line it with parchment paper.

7. In a pan, boil water mixed with baking soda in it. In this water, dip the pretzels for 30 seconds each.

8. Place these pretzels on the baking sheet. Brush them with the egg wash and sprinkle some coarse sea salt over them.

9. Put them into the oven and bake them for 20 minutes or until they turn golden brown.

10. In the meantime, boil the apple cider in a bowl till it turns syrupy. Then mix in brown sugar, heavy cream, and butter. Stir until the mix thickens.

11. Serve warm pretzels with the sauce.

Pretzels for Diet

A gluten-free diet. It sounds hard, but after going through this recipe, it won't continue to seem as such. This gluten-free recipe is the perfect fix for everyone who wants to have that perfect taste of pretzel all for themselves! Cook up this simple yet delicious gluten-free pretzel for when you get cravings because you and your taste buds deserve it!

Ingredients

For the Pretzels:

- Instant yeast – 1 tbsp
- Brown sugar – ¼ cup
- Tapioca starch – ¼ cup
- Xanthan gum – 1 ½ cup
- Kosher salt – 1 tsp
- Refined gluten-free flour – 3 cups
- Butter(unsalted) – 4 tbsp
- Baking soda – ¼ tsp
- Cream of tartar – ¼ tsp
- Apple cider vinegar – 1 tsp
- Saco cultured buttermilk blend powder – ½ cup
- Warm milk – 13 oz
- Egg whites – 2
- Coarse sea salt - 2 tsp

For the sauce:

- Honey – 3 tbsp
- Mayonnaise – 6 tbsp
- Kosher salt – ¼ tsp
- Dijon mustard – 1 tbsp
- Dry mustard powder – ½ tsp

Serving Size: 8

Preparation time: 25 minutes

Instructions

1. Preheat the oven to 400°F.

2. In a stand mixer, place a bowl with tapioca starch, xanthan gum, cream of tartar, yeast, baking soda, brown sugar, buttermilk powder and flour added in it. Sprinkle in some salt and mix well. Then, add milk, egg whites, butter, and apple cider vinegar. Combine them at a medium-high to high speed, or till the dough pulls away from the bowl's surface.

3. Place the dough in a bowl smeared with oil. Cover it with a plastic wrap, and let it rest for 60 minutes.

4. Sprinkle some flour on a counter. Put the dough on it and divide it into eight equal parts. Now, roll these pieces into thin long ropes, and shape them into pretzel knots.

5. In a pan, boil water with baking soda in it. Meanwhile, take a baking sheet and line it with parchment paper.

6. Dip each of these in the boiling water for 30seconds. Then, place them on the baking sheet, and brush them with melted butter and sprinkle the coarse sea salt over them.

7. Put them in the oven and bake them for 15 minutes or until they have turned golden brown.

8. For the sauce, mix the ingredients in a bowl and combine them well.

9. Serve the pretzels with the sauce.

A Perfect Dinner Knot

Fixing up a quick dinner is something we all are familiar with. After all, cooking up dinner after a long day of work is hard, but it is definitely something we all need. That is exactly why you need this pretzel recipe in your life! These delicious pretzels will not only save you from having to stand in the kitchen for hours to cook up something but would also give your grumbling stomach a great relief!

Ingredients

- Crushed pretzels – 1 cup
- Onion powder – ¼ tsp
- Garlic powder – ¼ tsp
- Parmesan cheese – 2 tbsp
- Dried basil – 1 tsp
- Olive oil – 1 tbsp
- Minced garlic cloves – 2
- Cooking spray - 1
- Red pepper(crushed) - 4 tsp
- Salt and pepper - 2 tsp
- Skinless chicken breast – 5 oz
- Egg(beaten) – 1
- Serving Size: 2

Preparation time: 10 minutes

Instructions

1. Preheat the oven to 425°F.

2. In a bowl, mix oil, garlic, and egg.

3. Meanwhile, in a bowl mix onion powder, garlic powder, cheese, basil and the crushed pretzels along with red pepper.

4. Sprinkle salt and pepper over the chicken. Coat the chicken with oil and then with the pretzel mix by dipping the chicken in them one after the other.

5. Take a baking sheet and line it with parchment paper. Place the coated chicken on it. Pour in the extra pretzel mix on top of them and shower them with cooking spray.

6. Put them into the oven and bake them for approximately 20 minutes, or until they turn golden brown in color.

7. Serve hot!

PB&J Sand- Nah! PB & Honey Bites

Peanut butter and jam are one of those classic combos that everyone has tried at least once in their whole life. And we love it! It is simple, sweet, and delicious! That is exactly why you will love this pretzel recipe. Except, these pretzel bites are not as simple as a PB&J sandwich. These pretzel bites are further dipped into dark chocolate to make a combo that is definitely better than PB&J! Something you may agree on once you get a taste of these delicious delights.

Ingredients

- Honey – 1 tbsp
- Roasted and unsalted peanuts – 2 cups
- Dark Chocolate – ½ cup
- Honey Pretzel – 1 pack (7 oz)

Serving Size: 12

Preparation time: 30 minutes

Instructions

1. Take the bag of pretzels and crush the pretzels into small bites. Now add these pretzel bites in a food processor and blend along with honey. Work the food processor till the blend forms a dough.

2. Place the dough on a counter with flour lightly sprinkled on it. Divide the dough and roll each of these divisions into small balls. Now, place these balls on a baking sheet previously lined with parchment paper. Let it chill in the freezer for 15 minutes.

3. Meanwhile, in the food processor, add peanuts and process them until they turn into a thick paste.

4. In a bowl, add the dark chocolate and a little oil. Place this bowl in the microwave and let it melt completely.

5. Dip the pretzel balls in the melted dark chocolate and place them back on the baking sheet.

6. Pour the remaining dark chocolate over these pretzels and place them back into the freezer for 30 minutes.

7. Serve!

The Classic Cookie Knot

Milk and cookies- the breakfast that can undoubtedly bring out the child in you. A taste filled only with joy! So, why not add it into a pretzel? It sounds almost like a dream; a dream that you can now achieve by taking a few simple steps! So, warm up some milk, because these soft and delightful pretzels taste the best with it!

Ingredients

For cookies:

- Salted butter – 1 cup
- Salt – ½ tsp
- Baking soda – 1 tsp
- Refined flour – 2 ½ cup
- Vanilla extract – 3 tsp
- Eggs – 2
- Granulated sugar – ½ cup
- Brown sugar – 1 cup
- Chocolate chips – 2 cups

For pretzels:

- Refined flour – 5 cups
- Kosher salt – 1 ½ tsp
- Brown sugar – 2 tbsp
- Warm water – 1 ½ cup
- Active dry yeast – 2 ¼ tsp
- Egg(beaten) – 1
- Coarse sea salt - 2 tsp

Serving Size: 8

Preparation time: 20 minutes

Instructions

1. Preheat the oven to 425°F.

2. In the stand mixer, combine the yeast and brown sugar in water. Let it rest for five minutes, and then add soft wheat flour, salt, and brown sugar into the mix. Combine on low speed. Increase the speed once the dough has combined enough to medium. Mix the dough for further 5 minutes, or until the dough pulls away from the bowl's surface.

3. Place the dough in a bowl smeared with oil. Cover it with a plastic wrap, and let it rest for 60 minutes.

4. Take a bowl and mix in the baking soda, salt, and flour around 10 minutes before the 60-minute time ends. In this bowl, add in the granulated sugar, vanilla extract, butter, and brown sugar and mix for around 5 minutes. Pour in the eggs and beat well. While blending this mix, add in the chocolate chips and stir for a few minutes.

5. After the 60-minute mark, place the dough on a counter previously sprinkled with flour. Slice the dough in eight equal divisions and flatten these divisions into rectangles. Place a bit of the cooking dough on top of each of these rectangles and pinch them close. Now, carefully roll these into logs and shape them into pretzel knots.

6. In a pan, boil water with baking soda in it. Meanwhile, take a baking sheet and line it with parchment paper.

7. Dip each of these in the boiling water for 30 seconds. Then, place them on the baking sheet, and brush them with the egg wash and sprinkle coarse sea salt over them.

8. Place them into the oven and bake for around 20 minutes or until they turn golden in color.

9. Serve warm!

Coco Pretzels

Chocolate!!! Anything that has chocolate in it automatically becomes a favorite. Just like how these pretzels would become your and your family's favorite now. These chocolate chips pretzels are the perfect snack for when you want to have some quality time with your family, and they are extremely easy to bake! You could snack on those chocolate chips while you cook, it will be our secret.

Ingredients

- Refined flour – 4 ½ cups
- Active dry yeast – 2 ¼ tsp
- Butter – ½ stick
- Warm water – 1 ½ cup
- Sugar – 1 tbsp
- Kosher salt – 2 tsp
- Baking soda – 1 cup
- Chocolate chips – ½ cup
- Egg – 1
- Vegetable oil - 2 tbsp
- Pretzel salt – 1 pack

Serving Size: 8

Preparation time: 45 minutes

Instructions

1. Preheat the oven to 450°F.

2. In a bowl, mix salt, sugar, and yeast in water. Let rest for five minutes. Then add in the flour along with the butter. Mix them on low till they have combined well.

3. Add in the chocolate chips and continue mixing until the chocolate chips have completely been combined with the dough.

4. Place this dough in a bowl smeared with oil. Cover with a wrap, and let it rest for 60 minutes.

5. Sprinkle some flour on a counter, then place the dough on top of it. Divide the dough into eight equal parts.

6. Now, roll these divisions into 18-inch-long ropes. Then carefully twist the ends over each other and shape them into a pretzel knot.

7. In a pan, boil some water mixed in with baking soda. Meanwhile, take a baking sheet and line it with parchment paper.

8. Dip each of the pretzel knots into the boiling water for 30 seconds each. Place these pretzels on the baking sheet and brush them with the egg wash. Sprinkle some pretzel salt over them.

9. Place them into the oven. Bake for 15 minutes or until they turn golden brown.

10. Serve warm!

Pudding with A Twist

When it comes to dessert, pudding is always a good choice. And, when it comes to pudding, bread pudding is definitely the one to go to. So, turn to this recipe when you need to have that delicious, sweet, and salty combo of a pretzel and a pudding all in one baking session! It is quick to bake, and the result is absolutely delightful.

Ingredients

- Pretzel bread – 2 oz
- Sugar – 3 tbsp
- Milk – 1 cup
- Half and a half – ½ cup
- Vanilla – ¼ tsp
- Chocolate chips – ¼ cup
- Egg yolk – 2
- Butter - 2 tbsp

Serving Size: 2

Preparation time: 20 minutes

Instructions

1. Preheat the oven to 350°F.

2. Cut the pretzel bread into thin slices. Meanwhile, mix some sugar and egg yolk in a bowl for 3 minutes.

3. In a pan, mix in half and half, vanilla and milk. Heat on a medium flame. Let it simmer for a while. Pour this mix into the bowl containing the egg yolk and sugar. Whisk well.

4. Coat 2 ramekins with butter. Place the sliced pretzel bread on the bottom of the ramekins. Add in ¼ cup of chocolate chips and ¼ of the mixture from the bowl into these ramekins. Keep layering till the ramekin is filled.

5. Fill the baking dish with water till the ramekins are halfway submerged into it.

6. Place the baking dish into the oven for 55 minutes or until the top turns golden brown. Remove the ramekins from the dish.

7. Serve warm!

The Rollers

Pretzels are amazing! However, making that knot for the pretzel is not easy, especially when you are running low on time. Don't worry! These pretzel rolls will not only free you from the careful procedure of handling the dough, but it will also give you the same taste as a regular pretzel would!

Ingredients

- Refined flour – 4 cups
- Brown sugar – 1 tbsp
- Salt – 1 tsp
- Active dry yeast – 1 packet
- Warm water – 1 ½ cup
- Butter(unsalted) – ¼ cup
- Baking soda – ½ cup
- Water – 2 ½ quarts
- Coarse sea salt - 2 tsp
- Serving Size: 12

Preparation time: 90 minutes

Instructions

1. Preheat the oven to 400°F.

2. In the stand mixer, combine the yeast in water. Let it rest for one minute, and then add in the refined flour, salt, and brown sugar into the mix. Combine on low speed. Increase the speed once the dough has combined enough to medium. Mix the dough for further 5 minutes, or until the dough pulls away from the bowl's surface.

3. Place this dough in a bowl smeared with oil. Cover with a wrap, and let it rest for 60 minutes.

4. Sprinkle some flour on top of the counter and place the dough on top of it. Make 12 equal divisions of this dough. Roll these separate pieces into small circular balls.

5. In a pan, boil some water mixed in with baking soda. Meanwhile, take a baking sheet and line it with parchment paper.

6. Dip each of the pretzel knots into the boiling water for 30 seconds each. Place these pretzels on the baking sheet. Slightly slice the top of these rolls and brush them with melted butter. Sprinkle some coarse sea salt over them.

7. Place them into the oven. Bake for 30 minutes or until they turn golden brown.

8. Serve warm!

Keto bites

On a keto diet and still want to have a baked dish? Then these gluten-free, low carb keto pretzel bites are the one for you! These pretzel bites are easy to cook up and have the perfect softness and fluffiness to their dough. So, put on that apron and get ready to cook up some of these delicious bites!

Ingredients

- Superfine almond flour – 2 cups
- Baking powder – 1 tbsp
- Low moisture shredded mozzarella cheese – 3 cups
- Cream cheese – 2 oz
- Eggs – 3
- Coarse sea salt – 1 tbsp

Serving Size: 8

Preparation time: 20 minutes

Instructions

1. Preheat the oven to 400°F.

2. Mix the baking powder and almond flour in a bowl. Let it rest.

3. Meanwhile, add cream cheese in another bowl and cover it with mozzarella cheese. Melt the cheese in a microwave with an interval of 30 seconds. Stir in between these intervals. Continue the process for around 2 minutes, or until the cheese has completely melted.

4. Mix almond flour, two eggs, and cheese in a food processor till the dough is formed.

5. In an oil-smeared surface, place the dough and divide it into eight equal parts. Roll these divisions into long logs, and then cut them further into small pieces.

6. Take a baking sheet and place a parchment paper over it. Place the pretzel bites on the baking sheet and brush them with egg wash. Sprinkle some coarse sea salt over them.

7. Put them into the oven and bake for 15 minutes or until they turn golden brown.

8. Serve warm!

The Vegan's Pick

Being vegan is a choice! This choice should not leave you without any delicious snack to munch on, though. And what could be better than some sweet and salty pretzels! These big and doughy pretzels will give you the same taste as any normal pretzel would, so if you ever desire the taste that these German snacks are filled with, you know which recipe you should turn to! After all, having a good snack is a requirement, and dare I say- a need!

Ingredients

- Refined flour – 2 cups
- Canola oil – 2 tbsp
- Active dry yeast – ½ tbsp
- Maple syrup – 1 tbsp
- Water – ¾ cup
- Baking soda – 2 tbsp
- Warm water – 1 ½ quart
- Coarse sea salt - 2 tsp

Serving Size: 4

Preparation time: 60 minutes

Instructions

1. Preheat the oven to 450°F.

2. In a bowl, mix in the maple syrup and yeast with ¼ cup of warm water. Let it rest until the yeast starts foaming.

3. In the stand mixer, combine the previous yeast mix with the refined flour, salt, and water. Mix on low speed. Increase the speed once the dough has combined enough to medium. Mix the dough for further 5 minutes, or until the dough pulls away from the bowl's surface.

4. Place this dough in a bowl smeared with oil. Cover with a wrap, and let it rest for 60 minutes.

5. Sprinkle some flour on a counter, then place the dough on top of it. Divide the dough into eight equal parts.

6. Now, roll these divisions into 18 inch long ropes. Then carefully twist the ends over each other and shape them into a pretzel knot.

7. In a pan, boil some water mixed in with baking soda. Meanwhile, take a baking sheet and line it with parchment paper.

8. Dip each of the pretzel knots into the boiling water for 30 seconds each. Place these pretzels on the baking sheet and slice the top of these pretzels twice or thrice. Sprinkle some pretzel salt over them.

9. Place them into the oven. Bake for 15 minutes or until they turn golden brown.

10. Serve warm!

Breakfast Bites

Who doesn't love a quick yet delicious breakfast? And, as long as we are talking about delicious breakfast, it is mandatory to add peanut butter into the equation. After all, anything with peanut butter is time-saving and yet somehow gives out the best results. Just like this pretzel recipe! These dough and soft pretzel bites that are filled with melting peanut butter are going to be your next favorite breakfast snack! And just a side tip- Get some melted chocolate dip to enhance the taste!

Ingredients

- Refined flour – 5 cups
- Active dry yeast – 1 packet
- Brown sugar – 2 tbsp
- Kosher salt – 2 ½ tsp
- Warm water – 1 ½ cup
- Butter(unsalted) – ¾ cup
- Baking soda – ½ cup
- Water – 2 ½ quarts
- Canola oil- 2 tbsp.
- Melted chocolate (to dip in) - 1 cup
- Coarse sea salt - 2 tsp

Serving Size: 6

Preparation time: 70 minutes

Instructions

1. Preheat the oven to 425°F.

2. In the stand mixer, combine the yeast and brown sugar in water. Let it rest for five minutes, and then add soft wheat flour, salt, and melted butter into the mix. Combine on low speed. Increase the speed once the dough has combined enough to medium. Mix the dough for further 5 minutes, or until the dough pulls away from the bowl's surface.

3. Place this dough in a bowl smeared with oil. Cover with plastic wrap and let it rest for 60 minutes.

4. Meanwhile, line a baking sheet with waxed paper. With a tablespoon, take out small scoops of peanut butter and place them on the baking sheet. Put them in the freezer for half an hour.

5. Sprinkle some flour on the counter and put the dough on it. Divide the dough into eight equal parts. Roll each of these divisions into a 20-inch long rope, and further slice this rope into small pieces perfect for a small bite.

6. Flatten these small divisions, place one frozen peanut dots on each of this flattened dough and pinch them close.

7. In a pan, boil some water mixed in with baking soda.

8. Dip each of the pretzel bites into the boiling water for 30 seconds each. Place them on the baking sheet again. Brush them with melted butter and sprinkle some coarse sea salt over them.

9. Place them into the oven. Bake for 20 minutes or until they turn golden brown.

10. Serve warm, with melted chocolate if needed!

Vegan Heart

Being vegan does not mean that you need to forget about your sweet tooth! We all have our cravings, no matter what diet one follows. And, not giving into these cravings just doesn't sound right, does it? That is why this recipe is a godsend! These pretzels are soft, doughy, and give a naturally sweet taste, perfect for your sweet dessert cravings, and they are shaped into hearts!

Ingredients

- Maple syrup – 2 tbsp
- Unsweetened non-dairy milk – 1 cup
- Active dry yeast – 1 pack
- Bananas – 2
- Refined flour – 1 cup
- Whole wheat flour – 1 cup
- Natural peanut butter – ¼ cup
- Ground cinnamon – 1 & 1/8 tsp
- Ground nutmeg – ¼ tsp
- Salt – ½ tsp
- Water – 5 cups
- Vegetable oil – 1 tsp
- Baking soda – 5 tbsp
- Coarse sea salt - 2 tsp

Serving Size: 12

Preparation time: 30 minutes

Instructions

1. Preheat the oven to 450°F.

2. In a saucepan, heat the non-dairy milk until warm. Add in the maple syrup along with the yeast. Let it rest for ten minutes or until it starts to foam.

3. Take ¾ of this milk and crush the bananas into it. Add peanut butter in it and mix well. Stir in salt, cinnamon, nutmeg, and flour along with the yeast mix. Combine until the dough starts to form.

4. Sprinkle some flour on the surface. Place the dough on it and knead the dough for 10-15 minutes.

5. Place this dough in a bowl smeared with oil and cover it with a plastic wrap. Let it rest for 60 minutes or until the dough increases in its size.

6. Now, make eight equal divisions of this dough and roll these divisions into 18 inch long ropes. Then carefully twist the ends over each other and shape them into a heart.

7. In a pan, boil some water mixed in with baking soda. Meanwhile, take a baking sheet and line it with parchment paper.

8. In a bowl, mix together the cinnamon, salt, oil, coarse sea salt, and maple syrup.

9. Dip each of the pretzel knots into the boiling water for 30 seconds each. Place these pretzels on the baking sheet and slice the top of these pretzels twice or thrice. Brush them with the maple syrup mix.

10. Place them into the oven. Bake for 15 minutes or until they turn golden brown.

11. Serve warm!

The Herbal Knot

Pretzels are delicious as they are. However, they taste ravishing with just a few alterations made to the normal recipe. These pretzels are the perfect example of it. They are made following the same classic pretzel recipe, with the much-needed addition of herbs to give you the satisfaction of having the taste of salt and herbs all in one bite!

Ingredients

- Refined flour – 3 cups
- White whole wheat flour – 1 cup
- Salt – 1 ¼ tsp
- Yeast – 1 tbsp
- Water – ½ cup
- Milk – 1 cup
- Honey – 1 tbsp
- Dried parsley – ¼ tsp
- Dried oregano – ¼ tsp
- Dried basil – ¼ tsp
- Garlic powder – ½ tsp
- Baking soda – ¼ cup
- Water – 2 cups
- Sesame seeds - 2 tbsp
- Coarse sea salt - 2 tsp

Serving Size: 12

Preparation time: 90 minutes

Instructions

1. Preheat the oven to 450°F.

2. In a pan, warm the water and milk along with yeast and honey. Let it sit for five minutes, then add in salt, dried herbs, garlic powder, and flour. Knead until the dough has combined well.

3. Place this dough in a bowl smeared with oil. Cover with plastic wrap and let it rest for 60 minutes.

4. Now, make eight equal divisions of this dough and roll these divisions into 18 inch long ropes. Then carefully twist the ends over each other and shape them into a pretzel knot.

5. In a pan, boil some water mixed in with baking soda. Meanwhile, take a baking sheet and line it with parchment paper.

6. Dip each of the pretzel knots into the boiling water for 30 seconds each. Place these pretzels on the baking sheet and slice the top of these pretzels twice or thrice. Sprinkle some coarse sea salt, sesame seeds and poppy seeds over them.

7. Place them into the oven. Bake for 15 minutes or until they turn golden brown.

8. Serve warm!

The Perfect Appetizer

If you are one of those people who need to have a good appetizer to present before your guests, then this recipe is the one for you! So, the next time you have your guest coming over, remember to whip out this simple and easy recipe to make the most delicious appetizer ever!

Ingredients

- Shredded chicken – 1 cup
- Soft buttery pretzel mix – 1 pack
- Havarti cheese – 4 oz
- Ranch dressing - 2 tsp
- Buffalo wing sauce - 3 tbsp

Serving Size: 20

Preparation time: 50 minutes

Instructions

1. Preheat the oven to 400°F.

2. Make the pretzel dough according to the instructions given on the pack. Then, place it in the oil-smeared bowl and cover it with a plastic wrap.

3. Meanwhile, add the shredded chicken with the buffalo sauce, and mix well.

4. Sprinkle some flour on a surface and place the dough on it. Roll the dough into small balls that fit into your palm perfectly. Flatten these balls, and then add in the cheese and the shredded chicken mixed with the buffalo sauce. Carefully pinch the dough close.

5. In a pan, boil some water mixed in with baking soda. Meanwhile, take a baking sheet and line it with parchment paper.

6. Dip each of the rolls into the boiling water for 30 seconds each. Place them on the baking sheet.

7. Place them into the oven. Bake for 15 minutes or until they turn golden brown.

8. Serve warm with a dip of ranch dressing!

The Big Delight

Normal pretzels are amazing. We all love them! Now, imagine having the same soft and doughy pretzels- in a few sizes larger, though. After all, normal is good, but the bigger you make it, the more you'll be able to have in one go!

Ingredients

- Refined flour – 2 ¼ cups
- Kosher salt – 1 tsp
- Brown sugar – 3 tbsp
- Warm water – 2 ½ cup
- Milk – 1 cup
- Active dry yeast – 1 pack
- Baking soda – 1/3 cup
- Butter (unsalted) – 10 tbsp
- Coarse sea salt - 2 tsp

Serving Size: 6

Preparation time: 30 minutes

Instructions

1. Preheat the oven to 450°F.

2. Take a saucepan, and warm up some milk in it. In another bowl, add in the milk along with the yeast. Let it rest for 4-5 minutes. Now, pour in the flour, salt, butter, and brown sugar. Mix well.

3. Place this dough in a bowl smeared with oil. Cover with a plastic wrap, and let it rest for 60 minutes.

4. Sprinkle some flour on a counter. Then, place the dough on it and divide it into six equal pieces. Roll these separate pieces into 30-inch long ropes. Shape them into a pretzel knot.

5. In a pan, boil some water mixed in with baking soda. Meanwhile, take a baking sheet and line it with parchment paper.

6. Dip each of the rolls into the boiling water for 30 seconds each. Place them on the baking sheet and sprinkle them with coarse sea salt.

7. Put them into the oven and bake for 15 minutes or until they turn golden brown.

8. Now, dip these pretzels into a bowl of melted butter. Remove them and let the excess butter fall off.

9. For the sauce, mix the mustard, brown sugar, vinegar, and mayonnaise in a bowl. Place the bowl in the refrigerator.

10. Serve warm with the sauce!

Mini Coco Bites

Eating chocolates as a snack is something that we all do. After all, chocolate does not have or need any specific time. But chocolate with or in something is definitely needed! What better to put the chocolate in than pretzels? The salty and sweet taste provided by the pretzel will heighten to the max with the delicious Hershey's and M&M combo! So, bring out those packets of chocolate that you have and get ready to make this delicious combo!

Ingredients

- M&M milk chocolate – 50
- Square pretzel bites – 50
- Hershey's hugs – 50

Serving Size: 50

Preparation time: 20 minutes

Instructions

1. Preheat the oven to 200°F.

2. Take a baking sheet, and line it with parchment paper. Place the pretzels on the sheet, put one Hershey's hugs each on the pretzels.

3. Place the sheet in the oven and bake for 5 minutes.

4. Take the sheet out, and then place one M&M each on these Hershey's topped pretzels. Press the M&M's down carefully.

5. Put these pretzels into the freezer for approximately 10 minutes.

6. Serve, or store them for later!

The Classic Cheese Pretzel

Cheese!!!! Just the name of it is enough to have your mouth watering, isn't it? Especially if it is stuffed into something soft and doughy. Now, pizza is definitely a go-to when you think about cheese and dough, but we don't always have the time to bake a pizza. That is why this recipe is perfect for people who love cheese all stuffed into a dough, one which you can bite and get that delicious stretch of cheese oozing out! Especially from the sweet and savory pretzels!

Ingredients

- Refined flour – 4 ¼ cups
- Kosher salt – 2 tsp
- Sugar – 1 tbsp
- Warm water – 2 ½ cup
- Shredded cheddar cheese – 1 cup
- Active dry yeast – 2 ½ tsp
- Baking soda – 2/3 cup
- Butter(unsalted) – 3 ½ tbsp.
- Water – 2 quarts
- Egg wash – 1 egg yolk + 1 tbsp water
- Coarse sea salt - 2 tsp

Serving Size: 8

Preparation time: 90 minutes

Instructions

1. Preheat the oven to 400°F.

2. In the stand mixer, combine the yeast in water. Let it rest for one minute, and then add in the refined flour, salt and sugar into the mix. Combine on low speed. Increase the speed once the dough has combined enough to medium. Mix the dough for further 5 minutes, or until the dough pulls away from the bowl's surface.

3. Place this dough in a bowl smeared with oil. Cover with a wrap, and let it rest for 60 minutes.

4. Sprinkle some flour on top of the counter and place the dough on top of it. Make eight equal divisions of this dough. Roll these into 18-inch long logs. Flatten these logs, and then spread the cheddar cheese along their lengths. Pinch close, and carefully shape them into the pretzel knot.

5. In a pan, boil some water mixed in with baking soda. Meanwhile, take a baking sheet and line it with parchment paper.

6. Dip each of the rolls into the boiling water for 30 seconds each. Place them on the baking sheet and brush them with the egg wash. Sprinkle some coarse sea salt.

7. Put them into the oven and bake for 15 minutes or until they turn golden brown.

8. Serve warm!

Pretzel Pie

Dessert is the most important part of any meal. It does not matter if a person has a sweet tooth or not, if there is a pie placed in front of them, they will surely devour it. Especially if it is a strawberry pretzel pie!

Ingredients

- Melted butter – ½ cup
- Crushed pretzels – 1 ¼ cup
- Granulated sugar – ¼ cup
- Strawberry flavored gelatin – 1 pack
- Heavy cream – 1 ½ cup
- Boiling water – ¾ cup
- Powdered sugar – ¾ cup
- Lime peel(grated) – 1 tsp
- Lime juice – ¼ cup
- Slightly crushed strawberries – 2 cups

Serving Size: 8

Preparation time: 30 minutes

Instructions

1. In a bowl, mix in the crushed pretzels and granulated sugar along with the melted butter. Flatten this mix at the bottom of the pie plate.

2. In another bowl, mix the gelatin with boiling water until the gelatin has dissolved. Add in the lime juice and the lime peel. Put this bowl into the refrigerator for 60 minutes.

3. Now, in an electric mixer, beat the gelatin mix until it turns fluffy and thick. Repeat the process with the powdered sugar and whipped cream until it starts to foam.

4. Mix the crushed strawberries and the whipped cream into the gelatin mix. Pour this whole mix in the pie plate.

5. Refrigerate for eight hours.

6. Serve!

Pretzel cake

Cake is a food item that you can have any time, and anywhere. You will never know when you get the craving for it. That is exactly why this recipe is the one to keep! This pretzel cake is easy to make and requires just a few ingredients. So, the next time you desire to have some cake, whip out this recipe and start cooking!

Ingredients

- Crushed pretzels – ¾ cup
- Light treacle – 2 tbsp
- Milk chocolate – ½ cup
- Butter – 2 tbsp

Serving Size: 12

Preparation time: 20 minutes

Instructions

1. In a saucepan, add the water and let it boil. Place a heatproof bowl on the top of the saucepan. Add in the light treacle, butter and chocolate. Stir and let it melt.

2. Take the bowl off the saucepan, add in the crushed pretzels into the mix. Stir well.

3. Place the muffin cases in the muffin tin. Put 5 pretzels each in the muffin case in the form of a holder. Add in the previously made mix into these muffin cases.

4. Place the muffin tin in the refrigerator for 60 minutes.

5. Serve!

Conclusion

An easy and simple recipe for a delicious snack is something that we all desire to have. That is why having pretzel recipes with you is a must! Pretzels are easy to bake, they are delicious, and you can have them with any meal you desire. It is completely your choice! After all, these German baked goods are loved by everyone, even by the ingredients you have lying in your kitchen right now. So, if you ever desire to have a pizza, a caramelized apple, or any other delicious treat with the taste of pretzel blended with them, you can have it! They won't only be your favorite snack, though. Serve these pretzels to your guests, and you are bound to have a shared meal with them every once in a week. Be prepared!

About the Author

Ivy's mission is to share her recipes with the world. Even though she is not a professional cook she has always had that flair toward cooking. Her hands create magic. She can make even the simplest recipe tastes superb. Everyone who has tried her food has astounding their compliments was what made her think about writing recipes.

She wanted everyone to have a taste of her creations aside from close family and friends. So, deciding to write recipes was her winning decision. She isn't interested in popularity, but how many people have her recipes reached and touched people. Each recipe in her cookbooks is special and has a special meaning in her life. This means that each recipe is created with attention and love. Every ingredient carefully picked, every combination tried and tested.

Her mission started on her birthday about 9 years ago, when her guests couldn't stop prizing the food on the table. The next thing she did was organizing an event where chefs from restaurants were tasting her recipes. This event gave her the courage to start spreading her recipes.

She has written many cookbooks and she is still working on more. There is no end in the art of cooking; all you need is inspiration, love, and dedication.

Author's Afterthoughts

I am thankful for downloading this book and taking the time to read it. I know that you have learned a lot and you had a great time reading it. Writing books is the best way to share the skills I have with your and the best tips too.

I know that there are many books and choosing my book is amazing. I am thankful that you stopped and took time to decide. You made a great decision and I am sure that you enjoyed it.

I will be even happier if you provide honest feedback about my book. Feedbacks helped by growing and they still do. They help me to choose better content and new ideas. So, maybe your feedback can trigger an idea for my next book.

Thank you again

Sincerely

Ivy Hope

Made in the USA
Columbia, SC
09 November 2020